Break the Code

How Coaching Became the Shortcut I Never Knew I Needed

BY NATASHA JAMES
SELF-PUBLISHED BY NATASHA JAMES
BATON ROUGE, LOUISIANA

Dedicated to my loving and supportive husband Earnest James Jr.,
my kids Earnest, Natyra, Kinsley, Ian James,
and my Goddaughter Ladira J. Richardson

"For nothing will be impossible with God."
Luke 1:37

Welcome!

Welcome to Break the Code

When I started my entrepreneurial journey, I thought hard work alone would be the key to success. But over time, I realized that strategy, clarity, and mentorship were the missing pieces I needed. This workbook is born from that realization—the moment I discovered that coaching wasn't a luxury, it was the shortcut I never knew I needed.

Inside these pages, you'll find prompts designed to help you think deeper, align spiritually, and act strategically. This isn't just about growing a business—it's about breaking old patterns, renewing your mindset, and positioning yourself to receive what's next. Whether you're just starting out or ready to elevate, you're in the right place.

Let's break the code—together.

xo, Natasha J.

ISBN: 979-8-9990088-1-7
First Edition, 2025
Printed and bound in the United States of America

For more resources and coaching tools, visit:
www.TheCeoSpeaks.com

For I know the plans I have for you," declares the Lord, "plans to prosper you and not to harm you, plans to give you hope and a future."

– Jeremiah 29:11

What to Expect From this Workbook

This workbook is your self-guided coaching companion. Inside, you'll find:
- Reflection prompts designed to challenge your mindset and spark clarity
- Scriptures and spiritual checkpoints to align your journey with faith
- Strategy-driven sections to help you implement what you uncover
- Pages designed to unlock breakthroughs—not just check boxes

Use it at your own pace. Revisit pages that hit home. Pause when something feels heavy. There's no rush—only results.

NOTES SPACE

My Code-Breaking Vision
Sketch, write, or list what your breakthrough season looks like.
Think: business wins, personal healing, mindset shifts, spiritual
alignment.

_____

_____

_____

_____

_____

_____

_____

_____

_____

_____

_____

_____

_____

WHY COACHING MATTERS

There are many shifts that happen when you're serious about reaching your goals.
Check in with yourself in this section:

I am ready to receive honest
feedback to help me grow.

       Agree

       Disagree

       Seldom

I am willing to be held accountable for
the goals I set.

       Agree

       Disagree

       Seldom

I am open to learning new strategies
and letting go of what no longer
serves me.

       Agree

       Disagree

       Seldom

NOTES SPACE

_____

_____

_____

_____

_____

_____

_____

_____

_____

_____

_____

_____

_____

_____

Visualize It

Create a vision board or draw a mental picture of your 'next level.' What does it look like to live fully aligned with your goals and values?

_____

_____

_____

_____

_____

_____

_____

_____

_____

_____

_____

_____

_____

_____

_____

I am ready to explore the thoughts and patterns that may be holding me back.

Agree

Disagree

Seldom

I believe investing in coaching is an investment in my future, not an expense.

Agree

Disagree

Seldom

I am committed to taking consistent action even when motivation fades.

Agree

Disagree

Seldom

I understand that growth requires stretching outside of my comfort zone.

Agree

Disagree

Seldom

If you checked agree to all six questions continue reading

NOTES SPACE

His Word, My Response

Read one of the featured scriptures. What does God want you to know from this verse in this season? Write your Scripture | My Reflection | My Prayer.

_____

_____

_____

_____

_____

_____

_____

_____

_____

_____

_____

_____

_____

_____

Reason 1: Blind Spots

What blind spots are you ready to address?

What's one habit I know is slowing me down, but I keep excusing?

01

Where in my business am I avoiding making a clear decision?

02

What feedback have I ignored because it made me uncomfortable?

03

What area do I secretly feel insecure about but pretend I have under control?

04

NOTES SPACE

_____

_____

_____

_____

_____

_____

_____

_____

_____

_____

_____

_____

_____

_____

_____

_____

_____

Scripture Reflection (Choose Your Own)
Pick a scripture that speaks to you right now. Reflect on how it applies to your business journey. What is God telling you about your next step?

_____

_____

_____

_____

_____

_____

_____

_____

_____

_____

_____

_____

_____

_____

_____

"Plans fail for lack of counsel, but with many advisers they succeed."
— Proverbs 15:22

Reason 2: Accountability Self-Check

Growth requires not just vision — but consistent action.
Check in with yourself honestly:

I set clear, specific goals — not just
"wishful thinking" ones.

Agree

Disagree

Seldom

I review my goals and progress regularly,
not just when problems come up.

Agree

Disagree

Seldom

I follow through on my commitments
even when no one is watching.

Agree

Disagree

Seldom

From Insight to Action
Write down 1 step you'll take this week based on what you uncovered in this section.
Choose an area: Mindset | Business Strategy | Personal Growth | Spiritual Focus.

_____

_____

_____

_____

_____

_____

_____

_____

_____

_____

_____

_____

_____

_____

_____

I seek feedback from mentors, coaches, or peers to improve.

   Agree

   Disagree

   Seldom

I take ownership of mistakes without blaming outside circumstances.

   Agree

   Disagree

   Seldom

I celebrate my small wins along the way, not just the big milestones.

   Agree

   Disagree

   Seldom

I understand that growth requires stretching outside of my comfort zone.

   Agree

   Disagree

   Seldom

If you checked agree to all six questions continue reading

NOTES SPACE

Implementation Check-In
What did you actually implement from the insights you've written so far? What's working? What needs adjusting?

_____

_____

_____

_____

_____

_____

_____

_____

_____

_____

_____

_____

_____

_____

_____

"Two are better than one, because they have a good return for their labor: If either of them falls down, one can help the other up."
— Ecclesiastes 4:9-10

REASON 3: YOU MOVE FASTER WITH GUIDANCE

There's no prize for taking the longest route.
Coaching collapses your timeline – helping you skip
unnecessary mistakes and speed up your journey to success.

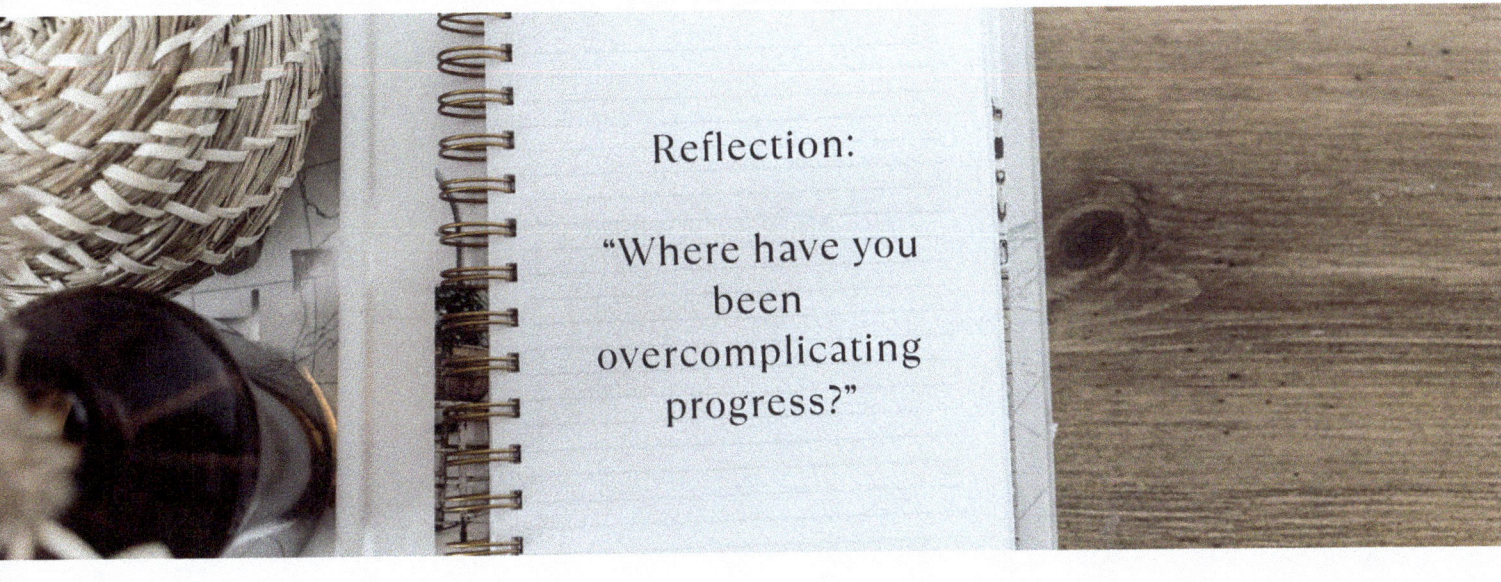

Reflection:

"Where have you been overcomplicating progress?"

PARTICULARS

Identify a major goal you want to achieve within the next 90 days.
(Target → What's the goal? |
Actual → Did you accomplish it?)

Choose a key habit you need to strengthen to reach that goal.
(Target → New habit to build |
Actual → Current consistency)

List one area where you will hold yourself more accountable starting today.
(Target → Accountability focus |
Actual → Progress update)

TARGET	ACTUAL

_____

_____

_____

_____

_____

_____

_____

_____

_____

_____

_____

_____

_____

_____

_____

_____

_____

_____

What Coaching Would Have Saved Me From...

List the moments, mistakes, or delays that coaching could have helped you avoid. Be honest about what you've learned the hard way.

_____

_____

_____

_____

_____

_____

_____

_____

_____

_____

_____

_____

_____

_____

REASON 4: CUSTOMIZED STRATEGIES BEAT COOKIE-CUTTER ADVICE

Your brand identity is the blueprint that shapes how people experience your business, trust your message, and choose your services.

How would you describe the overall look, feel, and personality of your brand?

What key emotions or experiences do you want your brand to create for your audience?

What words best capture the voice and tone of your brand?

If I Had a Coach Right Now, I'd Ask...
List 3 questions you'd ask a business coach today. What's confusing, frustrating, or blocking your growth?

_____

_____

_____

_____

_____

_____

_____

_____

_____

_____

_____

_____

_____

_____

_____

REASON 5: SUCCESS NEEDS SUPPORT

Behind every powerful brand is a collection of inspirations. In this section, you'll connect the pieces that bring your vision to life.

Books that shaped my mindset, leadership style, or entrepreneurial journey:

"The Alchemist," "Atomic Habits," "We Should All Be Millionaires,"

These are the fonts that resonate with me most:

(Example hint text:
"Playfair Display," "Montserrat," "Raleway," "Lora")

These are the colors that resonates with me most:
Colors that capture the energy and emotions I want my brand to express:

_____

_____

_____

_____

_____

_____

_____

_____

_____

_____

_____

_____

_____

_____

_____

_____

_____

The Breakthrough I Didn't Expect

What have you uncovered about yourself in this journey that surprised you? Describe the mindset shift or lesson you didn't see coming.

_____

_____

_____

_____

_____

_____

_____

_____

_____

_____

_____

_____

_____

_____

_____

_____

"As iron sharpens iron, so one person sharpens another."
— Proverbs 27:17

My Story
— Before Coaching

I started my first business
because I wanted more for
my life and my children.
I had a vision bigger than my
circumstances — but no clear
roadmap for how to get there.
Like so many first-generation
success stories, I learned to
survive through
determination.
I worked harder, sacrificed
more, and pushed through
the hard seasons.
But I didn't know how to
build with strategy — only
struggle.

MY STORY-
AFTER COACHING

Investing in coaching shifted everything.
I stopped operating from survival.
I started moving with clarity, structure, and faith.
Today, I've built multiple businesses, earned awards, put my kids through school, traveled the world, and created a life I once only dreamed about.

HOW TO FIND THE RIGHT COACH FOR YOU

✅ **Look for Alignment:** Choose someone who understands your values and respects your vision.

✅ **Look for Experience:** Work with someone who's already walked the path you're trying to travel.

✅ **Look for Chemistry:** You need someone who will challenge you — but also truly support your growth.

COACHING MYTHS VS REALITIES

❌ Myth: Coaching is only for beginners.
✅ Reality: The most successful people in the world have coaches.

❌ Myth: I should be able to do this on my own.
✅ Reality: Growth is faster and stronger with the right support.

❌ Myth: Coaching is too expensive.
✅ Reality: The right coach saves you far more in time, mistakes, and lost revenue.

FINAL THOUGHTS

You're not crazy for dreaming bigger.
You're not asking for too much.
You're not behind.
You're right on time — and you're closer than you think.
The only difference between struggling and soaring is the support you allow yourself to receive.

QUESTIONS?

www.theceospeaks.com

info@theceospeaks.com

THE ENTREPRENEUR'S PRAYER

God, thank You for the vision You've placed in my heart.
Strengthen me to walk boldly in the assignment You have given me.
Grant me wisdom to lead with excellence, patience to endure the process, and faith to keep moving even when the path isn't clear.
Surround me with wise counsel, sharpen my discernment, and let every step I take honor You.
I trust that the work You've begun in me, You will complete.
In Jesus' name,
Amen.

"He who began a good work in you will carry it on to completion until the day of Christ Jesus."
– Philippians 1:6

Thank you!

Thank you for investing your time, energy, and trust into this journey.
It means more than you know.
I created this guide because I believe in you — in your dreams, your vision, and your ability to build something extraordinary.

Success isn't reserved for a select few. It's available to anyone brave enough to show up, stay the course, and believe in what they carry inside.

If you take nothing else from this guide, take this:
You are closer than you think.
You are capable of more than you realize.
And you are absolutely worth everything you're working toward.
Thank you for allowing me to be part of your journey, even in this small way.

I'm rooting for you — today and always.

With gratitude and belief,
Natasha James

GOALS

WHEN SETTING GOALS, MAKE SURE IT FOLLOWS THE SMART STRUCTURE. USE THE QUESTIONS BELOW TO CREATE YOUR GOALS.

S	SPECIFIC WHAT DO I WANT TO ACCOMPLISH?	
M	MEASURABLE HOW WILL I KNOW WHEN IT IS ACCOMPLISHED?	
A	ACHIEVABLE HOW CAN THE GOAL BE ACCOMPLISHED?	
R	RELEVANT DOES THIS SEEM WORTHWHILE?	
T	TIME BOUND WHEN CAN I ACCOMPLISH THIS GOAL?	

PATTERNS I'M LEAVING BEHIND
WHAT MENTAL OR BEHAVIORAL PATTERNS HAVE KEPT YOU STUCK? LIST THEM. THEN DECLARE WHAT YOU'RE CHOOSING TO DO DIFFERENTLY MOVING FORWARD.

COACH YOURSELF THROUGH THIS
IF YOU WERE COACHING YOURSELF RIGHT NOW, WHAT WOULD YOU TELL YOURSELF? WRITE YOUR OWN COACHING ADVICE LIKE YOU'RE MENTORING YOUR PAST SELF.

_____

_____

_____

_____

_____

_____

_____

_____

_____

_____

_____

_____

_____

_____

_____

MY STRATEGIC GROWTH PLAN
WHAT 3 SPECIFIC AREAS OF YOUR BUSINESS OR LIFE NEED A COACHING
PLAN? EX: CLARITY | REVENUE | CONFIDENCE | HIRING | TIME MANAGEMENT.

_____

_____

_____

_____

_____

_____

_____

_____

_____

_____

_____

_____

_____

FINAL REFLECTION – I'VE BROKEN THE CODE
WRITE A LETTER TO YOUR FUTURE SELF FROM THE VERSION OF YOU WHO HAS ALREADY BROKEN THE CODE. WHAT CHANGED? WHAT DO YOU NOW KNOW TO BE TRUE?

_____

_____

_____

_____

_____

_____

_____

_____

_____

_____

_____

_____

_____

_____

_____

NOTES SPACE

_____

_____

_____

_____

_____

_____

_____

_____

_____

_____

_____

_____

_____

_____

_____

_____

_____

_____

NOTES SPACE

NOTES SPACE

NOTES SPACE

_____

_____

_____

_____

_____

_____

_____

_____

_____

_____

_____

_____

_____

_____

_____

_____

_____

NOTES SPACE

_____

_____

_____

_____

_____

_____

_____

_____

_____

_____

_____

_____

_____

_____

_____

_____

_____

Final Words
You made it to the end—but this is just the beginning.

If this workbook helped you uncover even one truth, shift one mindset, or gain one new insight—then it's already doing its job. But don't stop here. Revisit the sections. Keep asking better questions. And when you're ready for guidance beyond these pages, I'd love to support you.

You were never meant to figure it all out alone.

- Natasha James
@the_ceo_speaks | www.theceospeaks.com